Maidstone
TROLLEYBUSES

Robert J Harley

Number 4

MP Middleton Press

Cover Picture: A fine day in May 1966 sees LCD 52 at the stop outside Maidstone West Station. In the intervening years since this photo was taken this scene has been altered by mass demolition of buildings on the northern side of Broadway. Road widening and traffic congestion caused by a one way traffic scheme have also ensured that this seemingly peaceful view now belongs firmly to the past. (L.W.Rowe)

To Janet on the occasion of our sixteenth wedding anniversary

Published August 1997

ISBN 1 901706 00 1

© Middleton Press

Design Deborah Goodridge

Published by
   Middleton Press
   Easebourne Lane
   Midhurst, West Sussex
   GU29 9AZ
Tel: 01730 813169
Fax: 01730 812601

Printed & bound by Biddles Ltd,
   Guildford and Kings Lynn

CONTENTS

INTRODUCTION
AND
ACKNOWLEDGEMENTS

I first started to visit Maidstone at the end of the 1950s, and later, accompanied by schoolfriends Richard Grover and Roger Lane, I was able to observe at first hand the reliable and environmentally friendly trolleybus service. The pictures in this book bring back memories of a much loved form of transport, now sadly missed. Two abiding impressions of the trolleybus system were the smart brown and cream livery and the vehicles themselves, which seemed to glide effortlessly through the shopping streets and then accelerate silently out over the hills to the edges of the Kentish countryside.

In assembling the material for this book I am very grateful to all those photographers whose names appear in the caption texts; in particular I would like to thank Richard Rosa, Dave Jones, Chris Newman, David Padgham, Bob Cook, Lyndon Rowe, Gerald Druce, John Meredith and Stan Letts for their general assistance in locating suitable views. Rolling stock plans have been generously supplied by Terry Russell. My sincere apologies go to anyone whose name I have inadvertently omitted; unfortunately, I have not been able to trace some of the photographers whose work appears in these pages. I have tried to select views which have not been published in previous works. I have no hesitation in recommending *The Maidstone Trolleybus* by D.J.S.Scotney, *The Trolleybuses of Maidstone* by Daniel Kain and Malcolm Coates, and *75 Years of Municipal Transport in Maidstone* by the M&D and East Kent Bus Club to all those who wish to learn the story of these fascinating vehicles in greater technical detail. Readers are also reminded that the tramway era in the town has been documented in companion Middleton Press album, *Maidstone and Chatham Tramways.*

I would like to record my thanks to my father-in-law, Ray Oxley, who passed a critical eye over the photographs of his home town. As ever, I am exceedingly grateful for the support of my wife, Janet and the understanding of the rest of my family, in particular my children, Matthew, Abigail and Rachel.

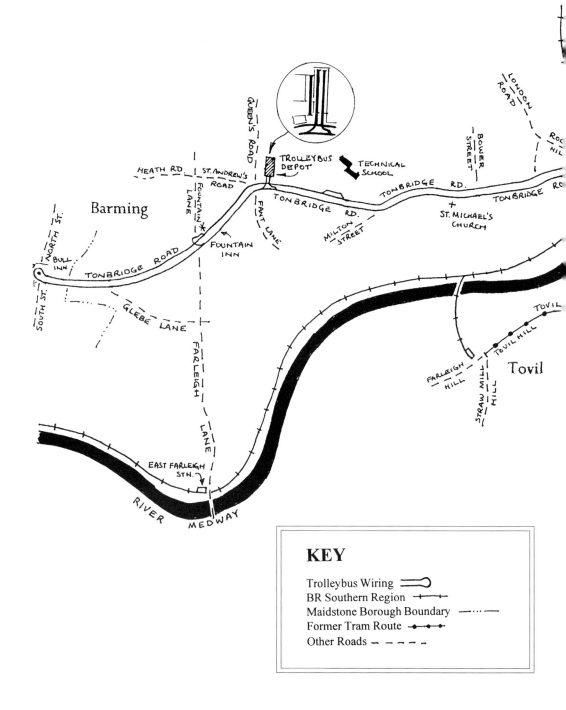

Barming

HEATH RD. ST. ANDREW'S ROAD

QUEEN'S ROAD

TROLLEYBUS DEPOT

TECHNICAL SCHOOL

LONDON ROAD

ROC HIL

BOWER STREET

FOUNTAIN LANE

FANT LANE

TONBRIDGE RD.

TONBRIDGE RD.

TONBRIDGE RO

TONBRIDGE ROAD

MILTON STREET

ST. MICHAEL'S CHURCH

NORTH ST.

BULL INN

SOUTH ST.

FOUNTAIN INN

GLEBE LANE

FARLEIGH LANE

FARLEIGH HILL

STRAW MILL HILL

TOVIL HILL

TOVIL

Tovil

EAST FARLEIGH STN.

RIVER MEDWAY

KEY

Trolleybus Wiring
BR Southern Region
Maidstone Borough Boundary
Former Tram Route
Other Roads

BY = Broadway
MW = Maidstone West Stn.

One Mile

GEOGRAPHICAL SETTING

Maidstone, the county town of Kent lies on the River Medway. Important road and rail links serve the town and many streets lead from the town centre up the valley sides to the suburbs which border the fine landscape of the Kentish Weald.

QUEEN'S MONUMENT
WEEK ST.
KING ST.
HIGH ST.
GABRIEL'S HILL
MILL ST.
PALACE AVE.
LOWER STONE ST.
MOTE ROAD
KNIGHTRIDER STREET
WREN'S CROSS
COLLEGE RD.
HAYLE RD.
UPPER STONE STREET
WATERLOO ST.

BW = BISHOPS WAY

ARMSTRONG ROAD
PLAINS AVENUE
LOOSE ROAD

Wheatsheaf

SUTTON RD.

LOOSE ROAD
PHEASANT LANE
NORTHUMBERLAND ROAD
NOTTINGHAM AVE.

CRIPPLE STREET
BOUGHTON LANE
GROVE ROAD

PAYNES LANE

SUTTON ROAD

LOOSE ROAD
LOOSE TRAM DEPOT
PICKERING ST.

WALLIS AVE.
BELL ROAD
LANE
HOLLINGWORTH ROAD

Parkwood

WALLIS AVE.

BRISHING LANE

KING'S ARMS
Loose
LOOSE HILL
LINTON ROAD

HISTORICAL BACKGROUND

Electric traction came to the streets of Maidstone with the inauguration in 1904 of the first tram route from High Street to Barming where the depot was situated. Subsequent extensions to Tovil and Loose (pronounced 'Looz') completed the system which then settled down to a useful existence until the 1920s, when the spectre of motor bus competition and the expense of fleet renewals and track repairs caused the Corporation to rethink its transport strategy. In the minds of many of the elected representatives the electric trolleybus offered the best solution to replace the trams. Thus it was that on 1st May 1928 the new "trackless trolley vehicles" ousted their rail-bound predecessors on the High Street to Barming route. Reaction from the travelling public was positive, however, it was not deemed economically viable to erect new trolleybus overhead on the Tovil route, and this service went over to motor buses on 1st August 1929. Loose Road was converted to trolleybuses on 11th February 1930 and this ended tramway operation in the town. A new section along Sutton Road was also opened and this formed part of a through service whereby vehicles from Loose and Sutton Road would cross town to terminate at Barming.

In the 1930s much suburban development occurred along trolleybus served roads and this influx of new customers boosted traffic receipts. During the Second World War the town was targeted several times by enemy aircraft and throughout the autumn of 1940 the overhead wire crews had a busy time repairing bomb damaged sections. With the end of hostilities in 1945 thoughts turned to acquiring new vehicles and to extending the system. On 22nd May 1947 the route between Barming Fountain Inn along Tonbridge Road to the Bull Inn was opened for passengers. In the late 1940s the basic service worked by each trolleybus was: Bull Inn to Loose, return to the Fountain, then to Sutton Road and back to the Bull. A bright future seemed assured for the undertaking as the wires pushed out along Sutton Road to cater for the new housing schemes. Trolleybuses reached Nottingham Avenue from the erstwhile Grove Road terminus on 21st June 1954; Brishing Lane, Park Wood was connected to the Sutton Road route on 4th May 1959. Finally, the full loop around Park Wood estate was opened on 19th August 1963. Inspite of the success of the trolleybuses, events elsewhere in the country influenced the council and an official announcement in 1964 confirmed the abandonment decision. However, one last new piece of wiring was opened on 13th December 1964 when the one way section in Bishops Way replaced the earlier route in Mill Street. The end came on 15th April 1967 when diesel buses took over the service.

Timetable extracts in this book are taken from the Maidstone Corporation Transport 16th January 1966 Timetable and Faretable.

```
                       FARE TABLES
          LOOSE—PARK WOOD ESTATE—BARMING
Stage No.                    K113/20
 3  LOOSE
 4  3  Walnut Tree
 5  3  3  Papermakers or Anglesey Avenue
 6  4  3· 3  Swan

 2  .. .. .. ..  Park Wood Estate
 3  .. .. .. ..  3  Bell Road
 4  .. .. .. ..  4  3  Nottingham Avenue
 5  .. .. .. ..  5  4  3  Grove Road
 6  .. .. .. ..  5  5  4  3  Cemetery Gates

 7  5  4  4  3  6  5  5  4  3  Wheatsheaf
 8  5  5  4  4  6  6  5  4  3  3  Plains Avenue
 9  6  5  5  5  7  6  6  5  4  4  3  Barton Road
10  6  6  5  5  7  7  6  6  5  4  4  3  Wrens Cross
11  7  6  6  6  8  7  7  6  5  5  5  4  3  High Street (Bishops Way or Queen's Mo.)
12  7  7  6  6  8  7  7  6  6  5  5  4  4  3  West Station

13  7  7  7  6  8  7  7  7  6  6  6  5  4  4  3  Bower Street
14  7  7  7  9  8  7  7  7  7  6  6  5  5  4  3  Milton Street
15  8  8  7  7  9  8  8  7  7  7  7  6  6  5  5  4  3  Western Road
16  9  9  8  7  9  9  9  8  7  7  7  6  6  5  5  4  3  Fountain
17  9  9  9  8 10  9  9  9  9  8  7  7  6  6  6  5  4  3  Glebe Lane
18  9  9  9  9 10 10  9  9  8  8  7  7  7  6  6  5  5  4  3  BULL
```

TRAM TO TROLLEYBUS

1. It is the summer of 1904 and Maidstone High Street by the Queen's Monument is the setting for this view of newly delivered tramcar 5. (R.Rosa Coll.)

2. Two new trolleybuses are being shown off at the foot of the High Street by the Medway Bridge. Aside from the publicity value of this display, the serious business of deflection/weight tests was carried out later on the bridge.   (R.Cook Coll.)

3. Tuesday, 1st May 1928 saw the inauguration of the High Street to Barming trolleybus service. Just prior to the opening the whole fleet was lined up for this photograph. Access to the depot for the remaining trams was by means of this single track in Tonbridge Road.
(Tramway & Railway World)

BARMING:
BULL INN TO FOUNTAIN INN

4. The peace of a tranquil day in May 1952 is barely troubled by the arrival of the trolleybus from town. After the vehicle has looped round the War Memorial outside the Bull Inn, the noontime slumber will return to Tonbridge Road. (A.J.Watkins)

5. Today's safety experts would probably have apoplexy seeing the three lads on the open back platform of trolleybus 73. However, in September 1958 it was all part of the fun of being a kid! Note the stone steps leading to the War Memorial. (L.W.Rowe)

6. The end is nigh for electric traction, and as if to rub it in, a new Leyland Atlantean monopolises the terminal stand. The diesel bus is painted in what can only be described as "faded denim" livery! This was a truly appalling shade of light blue which was a very poor substitute for the traditional Maidstone golden ochre/brown and cream. (I.Clark)

7. Trolley 71 basks in the sunshine of a fine October day in 1964. Opinions seem to vary as to whether the destination PARKWOOD should be written as one or two words. Contemporary (1997) buses seem to favour the latter interpretation. (R.J.Harley)

8. The last week of operation saw HKR 11 appropriately decorated for the funeral festivities. Also in this picture we can glance across the road and down South Street into the valley of the River Medway. (J.H.Meredith)

———————▶

9. A final look at Barming terminus one afternoon in October 1964 reveals an empty vehicle waiting for the return to town. Soon the school bell will be sounding and the reliable trolleybuses will be called upon once again to transport hundreds homeward bound. (R.J.Harley)

———————▶

10. Autumn has turned into winter. At the town boundary between Barming and Maidstone the benefits of electric traction are obvious, as the few hardy souls who have ventured out are carried safely along Tonbridge Road. No sign here of wheel spin or clouds of diesel fumes - just quiet, efficient service. (I.Clark)

11. The crossroads at Tonbridge Road and Fountain Lane is now a busy intersection controlled by traffic lights. All this was in the future as a smart looking 55 glides past the photographer. The AA sign LONDON directs motorists to Hermitage Lane and the main A20; note the fine collection of period motor vehicles parked outside the Fountain in this scene dated 24th March 1962. (L.W.Rowe)

12. Ex-Brighton trolley 51 is "on the loop" as the driver wrestles with the steering wheel to bring his charge round to the terminal stand. Passengers were not normally carried on this manoeuvre, and the conductor would say to eager young enthusiasts, the author among them - "Sorry, we're not insured to take you round this one!" (I.Clark)

13. The turn is almost completed, but the indicator on 72 is still going. The white line marks the boundary - left side, trolleybus - right side, pub car park. (C.Carter)

14. The rather basic passenger shelter would not seem to offer much protection from driving wind and rain; no doubt, waiting for a trolleybus in winter was a sobering experience for late night revellers from the nearby Fountain Inn. However, on this occasion the balmy breezes of summer prevale as 63 waits for its front indicator to be changed. (I.Clark)

15. The driver of HKR 2 turns his head to check on passengers in this view dated 13th September 1958. Hillman Minx UKP 661 is parked on the corner of Terminus Road - so named because the trams once terminated opposite.   (L.W.Rowe)

16. We now look towards the almshouses adjacent to the Fountain Inn. Trolley 68 lays over whilst the crew take a few moments rest in the lower saloon. Those inhabitants of Maidstone who could afford more luxurious transportation are urged to buy their Jaguar car at Drake & Fletcher, the well known local firm, founded in 1898 and residing until 1972 at premises in Broadway on the trolleybus route. (I.Clark)

17. Trolley 23 is seen on 9th August 1946 near the end of its working life. The background overhead wiring indicates that the Bull extension has yet to be constructed. On a related subject, the pair of wires between the trolleybus and the front wall of the Fountain is a relic of the siding erected by the Corporation in 1942 as a fleet dispersal measure in case of air raid damage to the depot. Several vehicles were then parked overnight on the verge. (D.A.Thompson)

TONBRIDGE ROAD:
DEPOT TO MAIDSTONE WEST STATION

18. LCD 52 gained the nickname of "the goldfish" after its front panel was replaced in August 1963. Here it is seen on 20th October 1965 at the junction of Tonbridge Road, St.Andrew's Road, Queen's Road and Fant Lane. As at the Fountain, this location is now controlled by traffic signals.   (L.W.Rowe)

19. The same spot as the previous view, but the climate has now become distinctly chillier. The power feed carrying 600 volts DC to the overhead is clearly seen above trolleybus 72. Substations which supplied the current were located at Tonbridge Road Depot, Fairmeadow near the Medway Bridge, Wheatsheaf Junction and on the Sutton Road near Senacre School. (I.Clark)

20. The photographer has now positioned himself on the other side of the road facing the Cherry Tree public house. The driver of 72 still seems to be missing, perhaps he has disappeared into the depot for a reviving "cuppa"! (I.Clark)

21. This is an early view of KO 8893 as it passes T.Longley & Sons on the corner of Queen's Road. This vehicle is running only as far as the High Street - passengers to Loose or Tovil would have to change at the Cannon for a connecting tramcar. (R.Cook Coll.)

22. The Southern Counties Touring Society, a group of like minded transport enthusiasts, hired a Maidstone trolleybus on 14th March 1948. KR 352 can justifiably be described as well past its "sell by date" as it attempts the tight turn from Tonbridge Road past the depot gates. (J.Turley)

23. In contrast to the previous shot, we now observe 24 from the opposite side of the road. Note the difference in livery details with the sister vehicle depicted in illustration 17. (V.C.W.Randall)

24. Inside the depot the accommodation could be characterised as rather snug and intimate as this picture proves. This somewhat cramped state of affairs ultimately goaded the Corporation into action and the diesel bus fleet was moved in 1969 to a new, more spacious site at Armstrong Road. (I.Clark)

25. A last look inside the depot shows trams and trolleybuses sharing the same building. This arrangement lasted from 1928 to 1930 when the trams were scrapped on a siding near the Wheatsheaf. The old depot survives today, complete with tram tracks and overhead troughing for the former trolleybus wires. (R.J.Harley Coll.)

26. Two forms of electrically powered vehicles, the milk float and 1944 utility trolleybus, GKP 513, are caught on camera outside the depot. The driver is about to make the turn into the depot yard. (R.Marshall)

27. On the left of the picture is West Borough School which was built in 1907 and demolished in 1980. The passing trolleybus is LCD 51, which was built for Brighton in 1950, sold to Maidstone in 1959 and was scrapped in 1967. (L.W.Rowe Coll.)

28. Before the advent of vast streams of motor traffic the atmosphere on Tonbridge Road was quite pleasant as this view near Western Road demonstrates. Trolleybus 83 is seen in the mid-1950s shortly after entering service with Maidstone. This vehicle had previously worked on the Llanelli system until abandonment in 1952. (S.E.Letts)

—————————▶

29. Many of the local big-wigs lived in large houses set back from Tonbridge Road. Whether the Sharp family, of toffee and sweet manufacturing fame, made use of the convenient trolleybus by the front gate is not recorded. A brand new Ransomes, Sims & Jeffries vehicle of 1928 is pictured near St.Michael's Church. (R.Cook Coll.)

—————————▶

30. The passengers on 18 might be reflecting on how much more comfortable the ride is now that the Barming trams have been withdrawn. In the distance another trolleybus waits at the approximate site of the former tramway loop. This exact location is also depicted in companion volume *Maidstone and Chatham Tramways*. (R.J.Harley Coll.)

31. Trolley 71 is seen on the descent to Maidstone West Station. Nowadays this stretch of road is one way in a westerly direction; this traffic scheme was introduced shortly after the trolleybuses departed. It was long claimed that, being wirebound, the trolleybuses were inflexible and held up necessary traffic "improvements", however, such speeding up as did occur was later largely negated by the sheer volume of private cars and heavy goods vehicles. (M.Coull)

TOWN CENTRE

32. Maidstone Bridge, a three arched structure over the River Medway, was opened in August 1879. Coming towards us are two members of the 1928 fleet: trolleybus KO 8898 and a Tilling-Stevens motor bus en route for London Road. This latter vehicle was constructed in the town; the subsequent history of Tilling-Stevens mirrors the general decline of the British automotive industry. In 1952 the company was taken over by the Rootes Group, which was later absorbed by Chrysler. The works closed down in 1977.   (L.W.Rowe Coll.)

33. This picture is on the cusp, as it were, of town development, showing as it does the hideous concrete, multi storey car park, cheek-by-jowl with some of the older buildings of the town centre. Approaching is ex-Hastings trolleybus 87, which was transferred into Kent when the East Sussex seaside network breathed its last in 1959. The date is 1st May 1965. (J.H.Meredith)

————————▶

34. Another seaside visitor to the town is 51, formerly owned by Brighton Corporation. The silver painted traction standards already bear signs informing motorists of the parking meter zone. The traffic tail back and the tower crane on the horizon are ominous signs for the future. (L.W.Rowe)

35. Town Wharf, on the left of the picture, was once the home of Bradley, Taylor and Youngman, Agricultural Seedsmen. This was until the bulldozers moved in to create yet another patch of tarmac. We can date this view to the mid-1950s before the Sutton Road service was extended to Park Wood. At the time of this picture this was the A.20 trunk road from London to Folkestone. (R.Cook Coll.)

————————▶

36. This is a scene taken after the opening of Bishops Way in 1964. Trolley 68 emerges from the new thoroughfare and immediately slows so that the poles will not dewire on the frog joining the wires from High Street. In the years since this photo was taken, the whole area has been turned into one vast traffic roundabout. This was made possible by the opening in November 1978 of a second bridge over the river. (L.W.Rowe Coll.)

37. A reminder of how the eastern bank of the Medway looked before Bishops Way came on the scene. Bridge Wharf and the line of buildings in the centre of the picture were demolished to make way for the new highway. The date is 25th August 1962. (D.C.Padgham)

⎯⎯⎯⎯⎯▶

38. Local postcard publishers took the opportunity in the summer of 1928 to present the town in the most up-to-date light, hence the appearance of the new trolleybuses in this view of the western end of the High Street. Note that one centre wire has been retained for the trams and the double track here would be used intensively early morning for cars taking up duties on the Tovil and Loose services and late at night for depot runs. (R.Cook Coll.)

⎯⎯⎯⎯⎯▶

39. We look across the river towards Westborough and Broadway and note that the tram rails have now been removed. Shortly after the first trolleybus overhead was erected in late 1927, this section of the High Street was inundated when the River Medway burst its banks. The only public transport through the floods was provided by horse drawn carts. (J.H.Meredith Coll.)

40. A symbolic gesture by a Maidstone Corporation trolleybus as it overtakes a Maidstone & District bus of the type which replaced the trolleybuses in Hastings. Relations between the two operators were sometimes quite strained and the Corporation more than once threatened to extend its own services in direct competition with M&D. Rather ironically, the end of this tale of conflict resulted in complete victory for Maidstone & District, which now supplies most of the borough's transport needs. (R.F.Mack)

41. Horse, electric and internal combustion engine powered vehicles jostle for position in this lively scene taken around 1931. Out of shot on the right is the Cannon! Note also that the entrance to Mill Street is closed off whilst the tramlines are being lifted. The trolleybus in the centre has for some reason *two* rear number plates. (R.Cook Coll.)

TROLLEYBUS SERVICES
BARMING—PARK WOOD—LOOSE

SUNDAY

	am	am		am	am		am	am		am	am			pm		pm
BARMING, Bull.dep.	9 38	9 45			1005			1025			1045					1 22
Barming, Fountain dep.	9 41	9 48		9 58	1008		1018	1028		1038	1048			1 18		1 25
Depot	9 42	9 49		9 59	1009		1019	1029		1039	1049			1 19		1 26
Milton Street	9 45	9 52		1002	1012		1022	1032		1042	1052	then at the same times past each hour until		1 22		1 29
West Station	9 49	9 56		1006	1016		1026	1036		1046	1056			1 26		1 33
Queens Monument	9 55	9 58		1008	1018		1028	1038		1048	1058			1 28		1 35
Wheatsheaf	1000	1003		1013	1023		1033	1043		1053	1103			1 33		1 40
Grove Road		1006			1026			1046			1106					1 43
Nottingham Avenue		1008			1028			1048			1108					1 45
PARK WOOD..arr.		1012			1032			1052			1112					1 49
LOOSE ...... arr.	1005			1018			1038			1058				1 38		

	pm		pm		pm		pm		pm			pm	pm	pm
BARMING, Bull.dep.		1 37			1 52			2 07				1022	1030	1035
Barming, Fountain dep.	1 33	1 40		1 48	1 55		2 03	2 10				1025	1033	1038
Depot	1 34	1 41		1 49	1 56		2 04	2 11				1026	1034	1039
Milton Street	1 37	1 44		1 52	1 59		2 07	2 14	then at the same times past each hour until			1029	1037	1042
West Station	1 41	1 48		1 56	2 03		2 11	2 18				1033	1041	1046
Queens Monument	1 43	1 50		1 58	2 05		2 13	2 20				1035	1043	1048
Wheatsheaf	1 48	1 55		2 03	2 10		2 18	2 25				1040	1048	1053
Grove Road		1 58			2 13			2 28				1043		1056
Nottingham Avenue		2 00			2 15			2 30				1045		1058
PARK WOOD..arr.		2 04			2 19			2 34				1049		1100
LOOSE ...... arr.	1 53			2 08			2 23						1053	

DANCE ORGANISERS!
Arrange for a Corporation Bus to convey your patrons home — it will improve attendances

Particulars from the Transport Offices, 372 Tonbridge Road

42. We now find ourselves in company with trolley 88 at the top of the High Street. Hanging back a little are two members of the Corporation's diesel fleet. On this warm August Bank Holiday in 1959 some weary travellers have probably patronised the adjacent Red Lion to slake their thirsts. This particular hostelry was always referred to by locals as the "gin palace"! (D.C.Padgham)

43. Trolleybus 12 pauses during the early years of operation. This loop around Queen's Monument was the original town terminus until one way wiring was extended down Gabriels Hill for the Loose and Sutton Road services. The policeman standing next to the driver's cab is a member of the Maidstone Borough force which first went out on patrol in 1836 and was amalgamated with Kent County Constabulary in 1943. (R.Cook Coll.)

44. In 1928 the service interval on the Barming route was one vehicle about every eight minutes, so potential passengers could linger over their shopping without the fear of being stranded in town. Behind the trolleybus is one of the Corporation's motor buses on the London Road route which terminated at Little Buckland Lane. Subsequent route extensions brought the terminus to Grace Avenue and finally to Allington Way. (R.Cook Coll.)

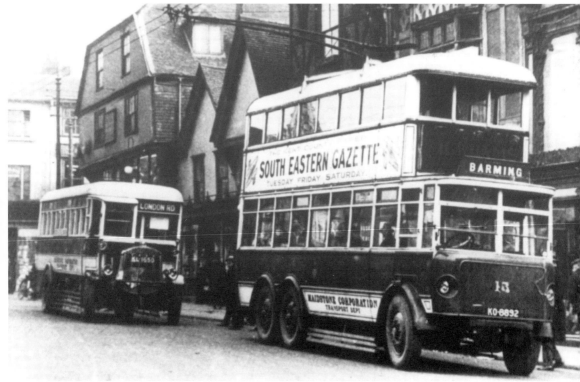

45. We survey the area around Queen's Monument from the roof of the Town Hall. Most of the buildings in the centre of the picture now no longer exist, having been swept away in the 1960s and 1970s by new shops and widened streets. However in this view, dated 3rd October 1954, we can still note the tower of Holy Trinity Church; nearer the ground, a Corporation motor bus heads off right down Gabriels Hill, to be followed shortly by a trolleybus on its way to Nottingham Avenue. (J.H.Meredith)

TROLLEYBUS SERVICES
LOOSE—PARK WOOD—BARMING

SATURDAY

	am	am	am	am	am	am	am	am	am	am	am	am	am	am	am	am	am	am
LOOSE ....dep.		6 00		6 20		6 34			6 50		7 00		7 12		7 22		7 32	
PARK WOOD..dep.	5 32		6 06		6 24		6 35	6 45		6 53		7 03		7 13		7 23		7 33
Nottingham Avenue	5 35		6 09		6 27		6 37	6 47		6 57		7 07		7 17		7 27		7 37
Grove Road	5 37		6 11		6 29		6 39	6 49		6 59		7 09		7 19		7 29		7 39
Wheatsheaf	5 40	6 05	6 14	6 25	6 32	6 39	6 42	6 52	6 55	7 02	7 05	7 12	7 17	7 22	7 27	7 32	7 37	7 42
Bishops Way	5 48	6 13	6 20	6 33	6 40	6 47	6 50	7 00	7 03	7 10	7 11	7 20	7 25	7 30	7 35	7 40	7 45	7 50
West Station	5 49	6 14	6 21	6 34	6 41	6 48	6 51	7 01	7 04	7 11	7 12	7 21	7 26	7 31	7 36	7 41	7 46	7 51
Milton Street	5 53	6 18	6 25	6 38	6 45	6 52	6 55	7 05	7 08	7 15	7 16	7 25	7 30	7 35	7 40	7 45	7 50	7 55
Depot	5 56	6 21	6 28	6 41	6 48	6 55	6 58	7 08	7 11	7 18	7 19	7 28	7 33	7 38	7 43	7 48	7 53	7 58
Barming, Fountain arr.	5 57	6 22	6 29	6 42	6 49	6 56	6 59	7 09	7 12	7 19	7 20	7 29	7 34	7 39	7 44	7 49	7 54	7 59
BARMING, Bull. arr.	5 59				6 59			7 15		7 23		7 37		7 47		7 57		

	am	am	am	am	am	am	am	am	am	am	am	am	am	am	am	am	am	am
LOOSE ....dep.	7 42		7 52		8 02		8 12			8 22		8 32		8 42			8 52	
PARK WOOD..dep.		7 43		7 53		8 03		8 13		8 23		8 33			8 43		8 53	
Nottingham Avenue		7 47		7 57		8 07		8 17		8 27		8 37			8 47		8 57	
Grove Road		7 49		7 59		8 09	8*15	8 19		8 29		8 39		8*45	8 49		8 59	
Wheatsheaf	7 47	7 52	7 57	8 02	8 07	8 12	8 17	8 18	8 22	8 27	8 32	8 37	8 42	8 47	8 48	8 52	8 57	9 02
Bishops Way	7 55	8 00	8 05	8 10	8 15	8 20	8 25		8 30	8 35	8 40	8 45	8 50	8 55		9 00	9 05	9 10
West Station	7 56	8 01	8 06	8 11	8 16	8 21	8 26		8 31	8 36	8 41	8 46	8 51	8 56		9 01	9 06	9 11
Milton Street	8 00	8 05	8 10	8 15	8 20	8 25	8 30		8 35	8 40	8 45	8 50	8 55	9 00		9 05	9 10	9 15
Depot	8 03	8 08	8 13	8 18	8 23	8 28	8 33		8 38	8 43	8 48	8 53	8 58	9 03		9 08	9 13	9 18
Barming, Fountain arr.	8 04	8 09	8 14	8 19	8 24	8 29	8 34		8 39	8 44	8 49	8 54	8 59	9 04		9 09	9 14	9 19
BARMING, Bull. arr.	8 07		8 17		8 27		8 37			8 47		8 57		9 07			9 17	

	am	am	am	am	am	am	am	am	am	am	am	am	am	am	am	am	
LOOSE ....dep.	9 02				912		922		9 32		9 42		9 52		1002		1012
PARK WOOD..dep.		9 03			9 13		9 23		9 33		9 43		9 53		1003		
Nottingham Avenue		9 07			9 17		9 27		9 37		9 47		9 57		1007		
Grove Road		9 09	912		9 19		9 29		9 39		9 49		9 59		1009		then at
Wheatsheaf	9 07	9 12	915	917	9 22	927	9 32	9 37	9 42	9 47	9 52	9 57	1002	1007	1012	1017	the same
Bishops Way	9 15	9 20	923	925	9 30	935	9 40	9 45	9 50	9 55	1000	1005	1010	1015	1020	1025	times past
West Station	9 16	9 21	924	926	9 31	936	9 41	9 46	9 51	9 56	1001	1006	1011	1016	1021	1026	each hour
Milton Street	9 20	9 25	928	930	9 35	940	9 45	9 50	9 55	1000	1005	1010	1015	1020	1025	1030	until
Depot	9 23	9 28	930	933	9 38	943	9 48	9 53	9 58	1003	1008	1013	1018	1023	1028	1033	
Barming, Fountain arr.	9 24	9 29		934	9 39	944	9 49	9 54	9 59	1004	1009	1014	1019	1024	1029	1034	
BARMING, Bull. arr.	9 27			937		947		9 57		1007		1017		1027		1037	

*—To Queens Monument.

46. Gabriels Hill was (and still is) a narrow street, but the pollution free trolleys seemed to fit in well, as can be seen here in this view. To the left of trolley 66 was once the site of the Palace Theatre, also known as the "Palace of Varieties". (J.E.Gready)

47. Above trolleybus 57 can be discerned the golden boot of the nearby shoe shop. This establishment with its imposing trade sign opened in 1790 and is still in business today. Another local firm, Fremlins, supplies the ales to the Ship Inn. The brewery was started in 1861 by Ralph Fremlin from Wateringbury. In 1967 it was absorbed into the Whitbread company. (R.Cook)

48. A repeat performance from 57 - this time going to Loose. Very close to this spot the River Len passes through a culvert under the road. Note that the time on the Granada House clock is R to N - in other words, ten to twelve! (I.Clark)

49. On 20th October 1965 trolley 52 passes along Lower Stone Street by the junction with Palace Avenue. The span wires carrying the overhead wiring have been anchored securely to the front facade of the Granada Cinema. (L.W.Rowe)

50. A year earlier than the previous view and we now approach the area known as Wren's Cross, and 85 is about to pull into the stop at which the future author of this book is standing. (R.J.Harley)

———————▶

51. The left set of wires diverges into Knightrider Street, but 68 will head straight ahead into Upper Stone Street. In the foreground is the site of the 7th August 1939 accident when trolley 29 overturned after skidding on a wet road surface. Fortunately the trolleybuses had a good safety record and such incidents were rare. (I.Clark)

———————▶

52. It would be unfair to caption this picture *...Trolleybus load of transport enthusiasts half way round the bend...* simply because many of these people had the foresight to record on film street scenes which have now vanished. So with a little more respect, we note a special tour negotiating the curve into Knightrider Street. Let us also note the splendid White Lion public house, now alas, also a mere memory. (I.Clark)

53. The former pub at the corner of Knightrider Street and Mill Street will eventually suffer the same fate as the White Lion. In the meantime the driver of trolley 70 is about to show a clean pair of heels to the pursuing Maidstone & District Leyland Atlantean as he accelerates into Mill Street, carefully avoiding the speeding Anglia van in the process. (R.J.Harley)

54. As BDY 807 moves away from the stop, we note in the background the former Archbishop's stables and tithe barn, built in the fourteenth century, which have been converted to house a carriage museum. The date is 7th April 1964. (L.W.Rowe)

55. A feast of antiquities - both ancient and not so ancient - are on view in this scene of Mill Street. Lovers of medieval architecture can contemplate the Archbishop's Palace and All Saints Church which was dedicated in 1395. Coming closer to the present day are the Corporation trolleybus and the front end of an M&D Atlantean. To the right of the trolleybus are the first two poles of the new Bishops Way extension and in the foreground a motorcycle enthusiast perched on THV 764 shows a late lamented name from British motorcycle history - ARIEL is printed on the back of his jacket. (C.Carter)

TROLLEYBUS SERVICES
BARMING—PARK WOOD—LOOSE

SATURDAY

	am	am	am	am	am	am	am	am	am	am	am	am	am	am	am	am	am	am
BARMING, Bull. dep.	5 08	5 34	....	5 52	6 00	....	....	6 18	....	6 25	....	6 35	....	6 45	....	6 55	....	7 05
Barming, Fountain dep.	5 10	5 37	5 43	5 55	6 03	6 10	....	6 21	6 26	6 28	6 33	6 38	6 43	6 48	6 53	6 58	7 03	7 08
Depot	5 11	5 38	5 44	5 56	6 04	6 11	6 12	6 22	6 27	6 29	6 34	6 39	6 44	6 49	6 54	6 59	7 04	7 09
Milton Street	5 13	5 40	5 47	5 58	6 06	6 14	6 15	6 25	6 30	6 32	6 37	6 42	6 47	6 52	6 57	7 02	7 07	7 12
West Station	5 17	5 44	5 51	6 02	6 10	6 18	6 19	6 29	6 34	6 36	6 41	6 46	6 51	6 56	7 01	7 06	7 11	7 16
Queens Monument	5 19	5 46	5 53	6 04	6 12	6 20	6 21	6 31	6 36	6 38	6 43	6 48	6 53	6 58	7 03	7 08	7 13	7 18
Wheatsheaf	5 24	5 51	5 58	6 09	6 17	6 25	6 26	6 36	6 41	6 43	6 48	6 53	6 58	7 03	7 08	7 13	7 18	7 23
Grove Road	5 26	....	6 01	....	6 19	....	6 29	6 39	....	6 46	....	6 56	....	7 06	....	7 16	....	7 26
Nottingham Avenue	5 28	....	6 03	....	6 21	....	6 31	6 41	....	6 48	....	6 58	....	7 08	....	7 18	....	7 28
PARK WOOD ..arr.	5 32	....	6 06	....	6 24	....	6 35	6 45	....	6 52	....	7 02	....	7 12	....	7 22	....	7 32
LOOSE ......arr.	....	5 56	....	6 14	....	6 30	....	....	6 46	....	6 53	....	7 03	....	7 13	....	7 23	....

	am	am	am	am	am	am	am	am	am	am	am	am	am	am	am	am	am	am
BARMING, Bull. dep.	....	7 15	....	7 25	....	7 35	....	7 45	....	....	7 55	....	....	8 05	....	....	8 15	....
Barming, Fountain dep.	7 13	7 18	7 23	7 28	7 33	7 38	7 43	7 48	7 53	....	7 58	....	8 03	8 08	8 13	....	8 18	8 23
Depot	7 14	7 19	7 24	7 29	7 34	7 39	7 44	7 49	7 54	7 56	7 59	....	8 04	8 09	8 14	....	8 19	8 24
Milton Street	7 17	7 22	7 27	7 32	7 37	7 42	7 47	7 52	7 57	7 59	8 02	....	8 07	8 12	8 17	....	8 22	8 27
West Station	7 21	7 26	7 31	7 36	7 41	7 46	7 51	7 56	8 01	8 03	8 06	....	8 11	8 16	8 21	....	8 26	8 31
Queens Monument	7 23	7 28	7 33	7 38	7 43	7 48	7 53	7 58	8 03	8 05	8 08	....	8 13	8 18	8 23	8 27	8 28	8 33
Wheatsheaf	7 28	7 33	7 38	7 43	7 48	7 53	7 58	8 03	8 08	8 10	8 13	....	8 18	8 23	8 28	8 32	8 33	8 38
Grove Road	....	7 36	....	7 46	....	7 56	....	8 06	....	8 13	8 16	....	8 26	....	8 35	8 36	....	
Nottingham Avenue	....	7 38	....	7 48	....	7 58	....	8 08	....	8 18	....	8 28	....	8 38	....			
PARK WOOD ..arr.	....	7 42	....	7 52	....	8 02	....	8 12	....	8 22	....	8 32	....	8 42	....			
LOOSE ......arr.	7 33	....	7 43	....	7 53	....	8 03	....	8 13	....	....	8 23	....	8 33	....	8 43		

	am	am	am	am	am	am	am	am	am	am	am	am	am	am	am	am	am
BARMING, Bull. dep.	8 25	....	8 35	....	8 45	....	....	8 55	....	....	9 05	....	9 15	....	....	9 25	....	9 35
Barming, Fountain dep.	8 28	8 33	8 38	8 43	8 48	....	8 53	8 58	....	9 03	9 08	9 13	9 18	9 23	9 28	9 33	9 38	9 43
Depot	8 29	8 34	8 39	8 44	8 49	....	8 54	8 59	....	9 04	9 09	9 14	9 19	9 24	9 29	9 34	9 39	9 44
Milton Street	8 32	8 37	8 42	8 47	8 52	....	8 57	9 02	....	9 07	9 12	9 17	9 22	9 27	9 32	9 37	9 42	9 47
West Station	8 36	8 41	8 46	8 51	8 56	....	9 01	9 06	....	9 11	9 16	9 21	9 26	9 31	9 36	9 41	9 46	9 51
Queens Monument	8 38	8 43	8 48	8 53	8 58	9 00	9 03	9 08	....	9 13	9 18	9 23	9 28	9 33	9 38	9 43	9 48	9 53
Wheatsheaf	8 43	8 48	8 53	8 58	9 03	9 05	9 08	9 13	....	9 18	9 23	9 28	9 33	9 38	9 43	9 48	9 53	9 58
Grove Road	8 46	....	8 56	....	9 06	9 08	....	9 16	....	9 26	....	9 36	....	9 46	....	9 56		
Nottingham Avenue	8 48	....	8 58	....	9 08	....	9 18	....	9 28	....	9 38	....	9 48	....	9 58			
PARK WOOD ..arr.	8 52	....	9 02	....	9 12	....	9 22	....	9 32	....	9 42	....	9 52	....	1002			
LOOSE ......arr.	....	8 53	....	9 03	....	9 13	....	9 23	....	9 33	....	9 43	....	9 53	....	1003		

56. Proof that trolleybuses can fit into a modern traffic scheme is demonstrated here on Bishops Way. In the background there is a line of Maidstone & District vehicles at the corner of Palace Avenue bus station. (C.Carter)

LOOSE—PARK WOOD—BARMING

	pm	pm	pm	pm	pm	pm	pm	pm	pm	pm	pm	pm	pm	pm	pm
LOOSE .... dep.	2 26			2 38		2 50		3 02		3 14		3 26		3 38	
PARK WOOD ..dep.		2 23	2 28		2 40		2 52		3 04		3 16		3 28		3 40
Nottingham Avenue..		2 27	2 32		2 44		2 56		3 08		3 20		3 32		3 44
Grove Road........		2 29	2 34		2 46		2 58		3 10		3 22		3 34		3 46
Wheatsheaf	2 31	2 32	2 37	2 43	2 49	2 55	3 01	3 07	3 13	3 19	3 25	3 31	3 37	3 43	3 49
Bishops Way........	2 39	2 40	2 45	2 51	2 57	3 03	3 09	3 15	3 21	3 27	3 33	3 39	3 45	3 51	3 57
West Station........	2 40	2 41	2 46	2 52	2 58	3 04	3 10	3 16	3 22	3 28	3 34	3 40	3 46	3 52	3 58
Milton Street........	2 44	2 45	2 50	2 56	3 02	3 08	3 14	3 20	3 26	3 32	3 38	3 44	3 50	3 56	4 02
Depot............	2 47	2 47	2 53	2 59	3 05	3 11	3 17	3 23	3 29	3 35	3 41	3 47	3 53	3 59	4 05
Barming, Fountain arr.	2 48		2 54	3 00	3 06	3 12	3 18	3 24	3 30	3 36	3 42	3 48	3 54	4 00	4 06
BARMING, Bull arr.	2 51			3 03		3 15		3 27		3 39		3 51		4 03	

	pm	pm	pm	pm	pm	pm	pm	pm	pm	pm	pm	pm	pm	pm
LOOSE .... dep.	3 50		†	4 02	††	4 12			4 22		4 32			4 42
PARK WOOD ..dep.		3 53			4 03			4 13		4 23		4 31	4 33	4 43
Nottingham Avenue..		3 57			4 07			4 17		4 27		4 35	4 37	4 47
Grove Road........		3 59			4 09			4 19		4 29		4 37	4 39	4 49
Wheatsheaf	3 55	4 02		4 07	4 12		4 17	4 22	4 27	4 32	4 37	4 40	4 42 4 47	4 52
Bishops Way........	4 03	4 10		4 15	4 20		4 25	4 30	4 35	4 40	4 45	4 48	4 50 4 55	5 00
West Station........	4 04	4 11	4 11	4 16	4 21	4 21	4 26	4 31	4 36	4 41	4 46	4 49	4 51 4 56	5 01
Milton Street........	4 08	4 15	4 15	4 20	4 25	4 25	4 30	4 35	4 40	4 45	4 50	4 53	4 55 5 00	5 05
Depot............	4 11	4 18	4 18	4 23	4 28	4 28	4 33	4 38	4 43	4 48	4 53	4 56	4 58 5 03	5 08
Barming, Fountain arr.	4 12	4 19	4 19	4 24	4 29	4 29	4 34	4 39	4 44	4 49	4 54	4 57	4 59 5 04	5 09
BARMING, Bull arr.	4 15			4 27			4 37		4 47		4 57		5 07	

	pm	pm	pm	pm	pm	pm	pm	pm	pm	pm	pm	pm	pm	pm	pm
LOOSE .... dep.	4 50		5 00		5 10			5 20	*		5 30				
PARK WOOD ..dep.		4 48	4 53		4 58	5 03		5 08	5 13		5 18		5 28	5 33	
Nottingham Avenue..		4 52	4 57		5 02	5 07		5 12	5 17		5 22	5 27	5 32	5 37	
Grove Road........		4 54	4 59		5 04	5 09		5 14	5 19		5 24	5 29	5 34	5 39	
Wheatsheaf	4 55	4 57	5 02	5 05	5 07	5 12	5 15	5 17	5 22	5 25	5 27	5 32	5 35	5 37	5 42
Bishops Way........	5 03	5 05	5 10	5 13	5 15	5 20	5 23	5 25	5 30	5 33	5 37	5 40	5 43	5 45	5 50
West Station........	5 04	5 06	5 11	5 14	5 16	5 21	5 24	5 26	5 31	5 34	5 38	5 41	5 44	5 46	5 51
Milton Street........	5 08	5 10	5 15	5 18	5 20	5 25	5 28	5 30	5 35	5 38	5 42	5 45	5 48	5 50	5 55
Depot............	5 11	5 13	5 18	5 21	5 23	5 28	5 31	5 33	5 38	5 41	5 45	5 48	5 51	5 53	5 58
Barming, Fountain arr.	5 12	5 14	5 19	5 22	5 24	5 29	5 32	5 34	5 39	5 42	5 46	5 49	5 52	5 54	5 59
BARMING, Bull arr.	5 15		5 25		5 35			5 45		5 49		5 55	5 57		

* To Queen's Monument

†—This Bus departs from Queens Monument 4.08 p.m.   ††—This Bus departs from Queens Monument 4.18 p.m.

57. An artistic and atmospheric scene unfolds as we peer through a stone gateway to observe a trolleybus crossing Maidstone Bridge. On the right a sister vehicle waits at Bishops Way. (R.Cook Coll.)

LOOSE ROAD: UPPER STONE STREET TO WHEATSHEAF

58. Upper Stone Street was really too narrow for two way traffic, and after the trolleys were abandoned, this whole stretch was made one way from town. In this early 1960s view LCD 52 climbs the hill past the corner of Brunswick Street East. Some of the buildings on the right were "rooming houses" of the most basic type. The property on the left side of the road has since been pulled down and much of it has been replaced by repair shops of the " Fit An Exhaust While U Wait" variety - such is progress! (R.Cook)

59. We continue to ascend Upper Stone Street to the Brenchley Arms where we catch sight of trolley 65 making light work of the gradient. At the time of writing the warehouses on the left were vacant and up for sale. (R.Cook)

60. At the risk of sounding like a pub crawler's guide, we now arrive at the Paper Makers Arms, where it seems trolleybus 87 has just missed the protruding first floor of a nearby building. Note that you could rent a black and white TV set for the princely sum of eight shillings and sixpence (42p) a week. (R.Cook)

61. On the far left of the picture is the junction with Old Tovil Road; in the centre is 26 still looking remarkably spritely for its age. The finial on the top of the traction standard was of a distinctive fluted urn design which dated from the tramway era. Many of these artifacts survived the trolleybuses and some can now be seen at the National Tramway Museum in Crich, Derbyshire. Others fell into private hands and the author recalls two which stood on the doorstep outside a cottage in North Street, Barming. (W.J.Haynes)

———————▶

62. This view is dated 4th June 1960 and shows 52 at the town end of Loose Road. Of particular interest to the technically minded is the spacing of the positive and negative running wires which was a narrow 15ins./381mm, as compared with the lefthand set which was fixed at the more normal 2ft./610mm. In the last decade of trolleybus operation the Corporation acquired much redundant overhead equipment from Brighton and was able to install spacer bars to modernise the wiring. (A.B.Cross)

———————▶

63. Increasing motor traffic is apparent in this picture of the changeover period from electric to diesel. In fact traffic has increased so much since this view that the pupils of South Borough School now require a footbridge to arrive safely at classes. (J.E.Gready)

64. A study in Kentishness reveals a group of oast houses by Plains Avenue and a Maidstone trolleybus on its way to Loose, where a short walk in the Garden of England would bring passengers to the hops and orchards for which the county is justifiably famous. (J.H.Meredith)

65. The oasts are in the background and the driver of trolley 54 concentrates on the approaching bifurcation of the Sutton Road and Loose routes. The open cab window testifies to the warm weather. (S.E.Letts)

TROLLEYBUS SERVICES
LOOSE—PARK WOOD—BARMING

MONDAY — FRIDAY

	am	am	am	am		am	am		am	am		am	am	am		am	am	am
LOOSE........ dep.		6 00		6 20				6 34			6 50				7 00		6 58	7 03
PARK WOOD ..dep.	5 32		6 06		6 24			6 35	6 45			6 53				7 02	7 07	
Nottingham Avenue..	5 35		6 09		6 27			6 37	6 47			6 57				7 04	7 09	
Grove Road.........	5 37		6 11		6 29	6*35		6 39	6 49		6 54	6 59				7 07	7 12	
Wheatsheaf	5 40	6 05	6 14	6 25	6 32	6 38	6 39	6 42	6 52	6 55	6 57	7 02		7 05	7 07	7 12	
Bishops Way	5 46	6 13	6 20	6 33	6 40		6 47	6 50	7 00	7 03	7 05	7 10		7 11	7 15	7 20	
West Station........	5 47	6 14	6 21	6 34	6 41		6 48	6 51	7 01	7 04	7 06	7 11		7 12	7 16	7 21	
Milton Street........	5 51	6 18	6 25	6 38	6 45		6 52	6 55	7 05	7 08	7 10	7 15		7 16	7 20	7 25	
Depot.............	5 54	6 21	6 28	6 41	6 48		6 55	6 58	7 08	7 11	7 13	7 18		7 19	7 23	7 28	
Barming, Fountain arr.	5 55	6 22	6 29	6 42	6 49		6 56	6 59	7 09	7 12	7 14	7 19		7 20	7 24	7 29	
BARMING, Bull arr.	5 58						6 59		7 15						7 27		

	am	am	am		am	am		am	am	am		am	am	am		am	am
LOOSE........ dep.	7 10				7 20		7 30			7 40				7 50			
PARK WOOD ..dep.		7 08	7 13		7 18	7 23		7 28	7 33		7 38		7 43		7 48	7 53	
Nottingham Avenue..		7 12	7 17		7 22	7 27		7 32	7 37		7 42		7 47		7 52	7 57	
Grove Road.........		7 14	7 19		7 24	7 29		7 34	7 39		7 44		7 49		7 54	7 59	
Wheatsheaf	7 15	7 17	7 22	7 25	7 27	7 32	7 35	7 37	7 42	7 45	7 47		7 52	7 57	7 58	8 02	
Bishops Way	7 23	7 25	7 30	7 33	7 35	7 40	7 43	7 45	7 50	7 53	7 55		8 00	8 03	8 05	8 10	
West Station........	7 24	7 26	7 31	7 34	7 36	7 41	7 44	7 46	7 51	7 54	7 56		8 01	8 04	8 06	8 11	
Milton Street........	7 28	7 30	7 35	7 38	7 40	7 45	7 48	7 50	7 55	7 58	8 00		8 05	8 08	8 10	8 15	
Depot.............	7 31	7 33	7 38	7 41	7 43	7 48	7 51	7 53	7 58	8 01	8 03		8 08	8 11	8 13	8 18	
Barming, Fountain arr.	7 32	7 34	7 39	7 42	7 44	7 49	7 52	7 54	7 59	8 02	8 04		8 09	8 12	8 14	8 19	
BARMING, Bull arr.		7 37			7 47		7 57			8 07				8 17			

	am		am	am	am	am	am		am	am	am	am	am		am	am
LOOSE........ dep.	8 00		8 07		8 10			8 20		8 30				8 37		
PARK WOOD ..dep.		7 58		8 03		8 08	8 13		8 18	8 23		8 28				8 33
Nottingham Avenue..		8 02		8 07		8 12	8 17		8 22	8 27		8 32				8 37
Grove Road.........		8 04		8 09		8 14	8 19		8 24	8 29		8 34			8 42	8 42
Wheatsheaf	8 05	8 07	8*12	8 12	8 15	8 17	8 22	8 25	8 27	8 32	8 35	8 37			8 50	8 50
Bishops Way	8 13	8 15		8 20	8 23	8 25	8 30	8 33	8 35	8 40	8 43	8 45	8 47		8 51	8 51
West Station........	8 14	8 16		8 21	8 24	8 26	8 31	8 34	8 36	8 41	8 44	8 46	8 48		8 55	8 55
Milton Street........	8 18	8 20		8 25	8 28	8 30	8 35	8 38	8 40	8 45	8 48	8 50	8 52		8 57	8 58
Depot.............	8 21	8 23		8 28	8 31	8 33	8 38	8 41	8 43	8 48	8 50	8 53	8 54			8 58
Barming, Fountain arr.	8 22	8 24		8 29	8 32	8 34	8 39	8 42	8 44	8 49		8 54				8 59
BARMING, Bull arr.		8 27			8 29		8 37			8 47		8 57				

*—To Queen's Monument.

66. The driver of 86 positions his vehicle for the turn at the Wheatsheaf roundabout. An indicator on the traction standard tells the driver and conductor that the overhead frog (points) is set for Loose. This automatic frog was usually set for Sutton Road, but an application of power by the driver of a trolleybus passing under an overhead contact would usual change the direction for Loose. Other frogs on the system were pull frogs operated by the conductor, the other automatic installation was situated at the Fountain. (I.Clark)

67. Trolleybus 89 is seen on the Wheafsheaf turning circle; it is operating an enthusiasts' tour on 21st August 1966. (L.W.Rowe)

LOOSE ROAD: WHEATSHEAF TO TERMINUS

68. CBX 532 has just negotiated the junction at the Wheatsheaf. It was here that a siding was constructed in 1930 to accommodate the last Maidstone trams. (S.E.Letts)

69. Just south of Boughton Lane the rather attractive Swan Inn is encountered. On the rear of rebodied trolleybus 58 the seating capacity is stated as 34 in the upper saloon and 28 in the lower saloon. In tramway days the track at this location was placed on the eastern side of the carriageway close by the inn sign. (J.E.Gready)

70. Semi-detached suburbia was in many ways the spiritual home of the trolleybus. In a typical 1930s setting between Norrington Road and Pickering Street trolley 71 scoots along with the front indicator already changed for the return journey. The date is October 1964. (R.J.Harley)

72. The same location as the previous view shows several trolleybuses stored out of service in the yard of Loose tram shed on the left. The date is 10th January 1966. Since this photo was taken, this area near Pickering Street has been built over. On Loose Road trolley 64 halts at the stop attached to a double bracket arm traction standard. (C.Carter)

71. One pole on, one pole off - the awaiting crowd of enthusiasts looks up admiringly, as well they might, because it was an art to get the trolley on the wire first time of trying. (I.Clark)

73. In its unrebuilt form 56 leads a Bedford OB coach along Loose Road. In this September 1953 view the semi-rural nature of this locality is still evident. (G.Druce)

74. Until July 1963 trolleybuses went in an anti-clockwise direction round the turning circle outside the Kings Arms, Loose. The conductor adopts a characteristic pose as trolley 70 runs under the crossing with the Maidstone bound wires. (S.E.Letts)

75. On 9th August 1946 a lad with a fishing rod gazes at 27 as a couple of passengers board. Note the bamboo pole hooked in place under the lower saloon windows. This was used after a dewirement to rescue errant poles. (D.A.Thompson)

76. Clear blue skies betoken a fine summer's day as a trolleybus waits in the dappled shade of an overhanging tree. Changes at this location today include the removal of the passenger shelter, and of course, Style and Winch ales are no longer served at the nearby inn. (S.E.Letts)

77. This picture was taken from the top deck of a trolleybus waiting to use the terminus. Before the vehicle in front departs, we can observe the springs necessary for maintaining the correct tension of the trolley poles. The two hooks at the rear of the roof were used for stowing the trolley poles. (R.J.Harley)

⟶

78. The sombre atmosphere mirrors the approach of the last week of trolleybus operation, however, 56 still looks capable of many years of useful revenue earning. Luckily, it escaped the mass scrappings and was later acquired for preservation by Mr.A.Stevens. (J.H.Meredith)

TROLLEYBUS SERVICES
BARMING—PARK WOOD—LOOSE

MONDAY — FRIDAY

then at the same times past each hour until

	pm	pm	pm	pm	pm	pm	pm	pm	pm	pm	pm	pm
BARMING, Bull dep.	1 55	2 00		2 12		2 24		2 36		2 48		2 57
Barming, Fountain dep.	1 58	2 03	2 09	2 15	2 21	2 27	2 33	2 39	2 45	2 51	2 57	
Depot	1 59	2 04	2 10	2 16	2 22	2 28	2 34	2 40	2 46	2 52	2 58	
Milton Street	2 02	2 07	2 13	2 19	2 25	2 31	2 37	2 43	2 49	2 55	3 01	
West Station	2 06	2 11	2 17	2 23	2 29	2 35	2 41	2 47	2 53	2 59	3 05	
Queen's Monument	2 08	2 13	2 19	2 25	2 31	2 37	2 43	2 49	2 55	3 01	3 07	
Wheatsheaf	2 13	2 18	2 24	2 30	2 36	2 42	2 48	2 54	3 00	3 06	3 12	
Grove Road	2 16	2 21		2 33		2 45		2 57		3 09		
Nottingham Avenue	2 18	2 23		2 35		2 47		2 59		3 11		
PARK WOOD arr.	2 22	2 27		2 39		2 51		3 03		3 15		
LOOSE arr.			2 29		2 41		2 53		3 05		3 17	

	pm	pm	pm	pm	pm	pm	pm	pm	pm	pm	pm	pm	pm	pm
BARMING, Bull dep.	3 00		3 12		3 25		3 35		3 45		3 55			
Barming, Fountain dep.	3 03	3 09	3 15	3 21	3 28	3 33	3 38	3 43	3 48	3 53	3 58		4 03	
Depot	3 04	3 10	3 16	3 22	3 29	3 34	3 39	3 44	3 49	3 54	3 59	3 59	4 04	4 08
Milton Street	3 07	3 13	3 19	3 25	3 32	3 37	3 42	3 47	3 52	3 57	4 02	4 02	4 07	4 11
West Station	3 11	3 17	3 23	3 29	3 36	3 41	3 46	3 51	3 56	4 01	4 06	4 06	4 11	4 15
Queen's Monument	3 13	3 19	3 25	3 31	3 38	3 43	3 48	3 53	3 58	4 03	4 08	4 08	4 13	4 17
Wheatsheaf	3 18	3 24	3 30	3 36	3 43	3 48	3 53	3 58	4 03	4 08	4 13		4 18	4 22
Grove Road	3 21		3 33		3 46		3 56		4 06		4 16		4 25	
Nottingham Avenue	3 23		3 35		3 48		3 58		4 08		4 18		4 27	
PARK WOOD arr.	3 27		3 39		3 52		4 02		4 12		4 22		4 31	
LOOSE arr.		3 29		3 41		3 53		4 03		4 13		4 23		

	pm	pm	pm	pm	pm	pm	pm	pm	pm	pm	pm	pm	pm	pm
BARMING, Bull dep.		4 05		4 15		4 25		4 35		4 45				
Barming, Fountain dep.	4 08		4 13	4 18	4 23	4 25	4 28	4 33	4 35	4 38	4 43	4 45	4 48	4 53
Depot	4 09	4 09	4 14	4 19	4 24	4 26	4 29	4 34	4 36	4 39	4 44	4 46	4 49	4 54
Milton Street	4 12	4 12	4 17	4 22	4 27	4 29	4 32	4 37	4 39	4 42	4 47	4 49	4 52	4 57
West Station	4 16	4 16	4 21	4 26	4 31	4 33	4 36	4 41	4 43	4 46	4 51	4 53	4 56	5 01
Queen's Monument	4 18	4 18	4 23	4 28	4 33	4 35	4 38	4 43	4 45	4 48	4 53	4 55	4 58	5 03
Wheatsheaf		4 23		4 28	4 33	4 38	4 40	4 43	4 48	4 50	4 53	4 58	5 00	5 03	5 08
Grove Road		4 26		4 36	4 41		4 46		4 56		5 06		5 11	
Nottingham Avenue		4 28		4 38	4 43		4 48	4 53		4 58	5 03		5 08	5 13
PARK WOOD arr.		4 32		4 42	4 47		4 52	4 57		5 02	5 07		5 12	5 17
LOOSE arr.			4 33			4 45			4 55			5 05		

SUTTON ROAD:
WHEATSHEAF TO PARK WOOD

79. The Sutton Road route opened up territory previously unserved by the trams. The 1930 trolleybus extension supplanted an earlier motor bus route which ran from the Cannon to Mangravet Avenue. The trolleybus shown here has just left the Wheatsheaf at the beginning of Sutton Road. (S.E.Letts)

80. This splendid line of trees survives to this day as a pleasant feature which enhances Sutton Road. On a fine day in the mid-1950s HKR 1 (which nowadays would probably qualify as a "cherished numberplate"!) has the road to itself. (S.E.Letts)

81. Trolleybus 52 is pictured at the stop by Grove Road. (I.Clark)

82. The conductress gets out to pull the frog as trolley 72 prepares to use the Grove Road turning circle. In the last years of the system two turns at 8.13am and 8.32am were scheduled here on Saturdays. (R.Cook)

83. Grove Road served as the terminus of the Sutton Road route from 12th February 1930 to 21st June 1954. The vehicle in this view stands on the edge of the town's housing development. (L.W.Rowe Coll.)

84. Nottingham Avenue was the end of the 1954 extension. Here trolley 70 lays over before the return to town.   (I.Clark)

———————→

85. We follow the fortunes of 70 as it edges out into Sutton Road on a short working to High Street, Queen's Monument.   (I.Clark)

———————→

86. On 3rd October 1954 there is little other traffic to disturb this trolleybus as it moves off from the terminus. Nowadays this area seems to be one constant flow of cars trying to get in and out of the adjacent Safeway superstore. (J.H.Meredith)

87. Appropriately this caption features the vehicle with the same fleet number. It has just turned right from the main Sutton Road into Wallis Avenue and has crossed the inbound loop wiring which emerges from Bell Road. The date is 13th March 1965. (L.W.Rowe)

88. On the same date as the previous picture, we go further into Park Wood to observe trolleybus 65 as it passes the entrance to Wrangleden Road. Note the single bracket arms supporting the overhead. (L.W.Rowe)

89. Trolley 72 passes the southern end of Wrangleden Road at a time before the school hedge had grown to maturity. (C.Carter)

90. Compare this view with the previous one - again we are looking west, but this time the estate is barely half finished, as 51 ferries participants on an enthusiasts' tour on 12th April 1959. The terminus at Brishing Lane is literally just round the corner, and public service opened on 4th May 1959, ironically just over two months to the day since Kent's only other trolleybus routes, the 654,696 and 698, were axed by London Transport. The whole extension from Nottingham Avenue to Brishing Lane cost £1,826 and much of the overhead equipment and the traction standards were purchased secondhand from Brighton Corporation. (J.H.Meredith)

91. At the far point of the loop in Wallis Avenue a trolleybus stops to pick up passengers. Plans to run an extended loop via Long Shaw Road, Selby Road and Bicknor Road never reached fruition, although the traction standards were actually erected to serve as street lights. (R.Cook)

92. Woodland still borders the estate as 72 passes the end of Hollingworth Road. (C.Carter)

93. In Bell Road some of the architecture is definitely 1960s, an era known for its functional public housing rather than its elegance of style. To be fair, Park Wood was laid out better than some of its contemporaries in other towns. Unfortunately, the local inhabitants do not now have the benefit of a pollution free trolleybus service. (M.Coull)

ROLLING STOCK

The Maidstone trolleybus fleet was divided into two types: the original six wheel "trackless trolley vehicles", and the later four wheelers. Livery in the trolleybus era was golden ochre/brown and white/cream, and as can be seen from the following photos, this colour scheme was applied over the years in different combinations.

94. Two Tilling-Stevens lorries are seen hard at work towing some of the new trolleybuses back to Maidstone. Leading vehicle, KO 8891, which was originally numbered 14 in the fleet, was part of a batch of eight vehicles delivered new in 1928. They were constructed by Ransomes, Sims & Jeffries at Ipswich. (R.Cook Coll.)

95. In this driver's side view we can note the position of the trolleypoles which were mounted "amidships" on a single trolleybase. The fleet name was in gold letters, shaded red. (R.Cook Coll.)

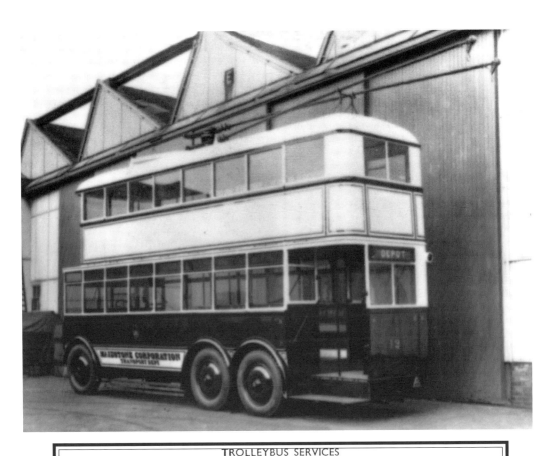

TROLLEYBUS SERVICES
BARMING—PARK WOOD—LOOSE

MONDAY — FRIDAY

	am	am	am		am	am	am		am	am	am		am	am	am		am	am
BARMING Bull dep.	5 08	5 34	....		5 52	6 00	....		....	6 18	....		6 25	....	....		....	6 35
Barming, Fountain dep.	5 10	5 37	5 43		5 55	6 03	6 10		....	6 21	....		6 26	6 28	6 33		....	6 35
Depot	5 11	5 38	5 44		5 56	6 04	6 11		6 12	6 16	6 22		6 27	6 29	6 34		....	6 36
Milton Street	5 13	5 40	5 46		5 58	6 06	6 14		6 15	6 19	6 25		6 30	6 32	6 37		....	6 39
West Station	5 17	5 44	5 50		6 02	6 10	6 18		6 19	6 23	6 29		6 34	6 36	6 41		....	6 43
Queen's Monument	5 19	5 46	5 52		6 04	6 12	6 20		6 21	6 25	6 31		6 36	6 38	6 43		6 45	6 45
Wheatsheaf	5 24	5 51	5 57		6 09	6 17	6 25		6 26	6 30	6 36		6 41	6 43	6 48		6 50	6 50
Grove Road	5 26	....	6 00		....	6 19	....		6 29	6 33	6 39		....	6 46	6 51		6 53	....
Nottingham Avenue	5 28	....	6 02		....	6 21	....		6 31	....	6 41		....	6 48	6 53		....	....
PARK WOOD arr.	5 32	....	6 06		....	6 24	....		6 35	....	6 45		....	6 52	6 57		....	....
LOOSE arr.	....	5 56	....		6 14	....	6 30		....	....	....		6 46	....	....		....	6 55

	am	am		am	am	am		am	am	am		am	am	am		am	am
BARMING Bull dep.	6 35	....		6 45	....	....		6 55	....	....		7 05	....	....		7 15	....
Barming, Fountain dep.	6 38	6 43		6 45	6 48	6 53		6 55	6 58	7 03		7 05	7 08	7 13		7 15	7 18	7 23
Depot	6 39	6 44		6 46	6 49	6 54		6 56	6 59	7 04		7 06	7 09	7 14		7 16	7 19	7 24
Milton Street	6 42	6 47		6 49	6 52	6 57		6 59	7 02	7 07		7 09	7 12	7 17		7 19	7 22	7 27
West Station	6 46	6 51		6 53	6 56	7 01		7 03	7 06	7 11		7 13	7 16	7 21		7 23	7 26	7 31
Queen's Monument	6 48	6 53		6 55	6 58	7 03		7 05	7 08	7 13		7 15	7 18	7 23		7 25	7 28	7 33
Wheatsheaf	6 53	6 58		7 00	7 03	7 08		7 10	7 13	7 18		7 20	7 23	7 28		7 30	7 33	7 38
Grove Road	6 56	7 01		....	7 06	7 11		....	7 16	7 21		....	7 26	7 31		....	7 36	7 41
Nottingham Avenue	6 58	7 03		....	7 08	7 13		....	7 18	7 23		....	7 28	7 33		....	7 38	7 43
PARK WOOD arr.	7 02	7 07		....	7 12	7 17		....	7 22	7 27		....	7 32	7 37		....	7 42	7 47
LOOSE arr.	....	....		7 05	....	....		7 15	....	....		7 25	....	....		7 35	....

	am	am	am		am	am	am		am	am	am		am	am	am		am	am
BARMING Bull dep.	....	7 25	....		....	7 35	....		....	7 45	....		....	7 55	....		....	....
Barming, Fountain dep.	7 25	7 28	7 33		....	7 35	7 38		....	7 43	7 45	7 48		7 53	7 55	7 58		8 03	8 05
Depot	7 26	7 29	7 34		....	7 36	7 39	7 41		7 44	7 46	7 49		7 54	7 56	7 59		8 04	8 06
Milton Street	7 29	7 32	7 37		....	7 39	7 42	7 44		7 47	7 49	7 52		7 57	7 59	8 02		8 07	8 09
West Station	7 33	7 36	7 41		....	7 43	7 46	7 48		7 51	7 53	7 56		8 01	8 03	8 06		8 11	8 13
Queen's Monument	7 35	7 38	7 43		....	7 45	7 48	7 50		7 53	7 55	7 58		8 03	8 05	8 08		8 13	8 15
Wheatsheaf	7 40	7 43	7 48		....	7 50	7 53	7 55		7 58	8 00	8 03		8 08	8 10	8 13		8 18	8 20
Grove Road	....	7 46	7 51		....	....	7 56		....	8 01	....	8 06		8 11	....	8 16		8 21	....
Nottingham Avenue	....	7 48	7 53		....	....	7 58		....	8 03	....	8 08		8 13	....	8 18		8 23	....
PARK WOOD arr.	....	7 52	7 57		....	....	8 02		....	8 07	....	8 12		8 17	....	8 22		8 27	....
LOOSE arr.	7 45	....	....		....	7 55	....	8 00		8 05	....	....		8 15	....	....		....	8 25

96. We look now at the passenger boarding side of trolleybus 12. Seating in the lower saloon was for 31 and in the upper saloon for 32. Note that 12 has yet to receive its numberplate, in fact, it has now been established that the depot staff sometimes swapped numberplates amongst different vehicles, so that the fleet number may not always tally with the registration.
(R.Cook Coll.)

97. This rear view of 13 shows the single stop light and some of the elaborate lining on the lower panel beneath the window with the indicator box. The lining out was with dark green and brown lines, and in the corners of the panels a gold floral device was affixed.
(Tramway & Railway World)

98. Trolleybus 15 shows HIGH STREET, but it is going nowhere as it has been dumped out of service. The 11 to 18 batch of vehicles was withdrawn in 1946/7. (J.H.Meredith)

99. We note the slightly different body styles of the leading Ransomes vehicle and a newer English Electric vehicle behind. The latter belonged to a batch of trolleybuses constructed by EE in 1930 and numbered in a series from 23 to 29. They were all withdrawn in 1946-48. (R.Rosa Coll.)

100. This excellent broadside view of one of the 23 to 29 vehicles shows a later livery, but the trolleypoles are still mounted on a single trolleybase. There were 30 seats in the upper saloon and 26 in the lower saloon. These vehicles were registered KR 351-357. (R.Cook Coll.)

101. Because of shortages during the Second World War, trolleybuses, furniture and a number of other products came in "utility" versions. Here is 58, a 1944 Sunbeam manufactured in Wolverhampton. It was part of a batch numbered 54 to 58, and featured a more modern twin trolleybase. Note the "blackout" masks for the headlights. (R.Cook Coll.)

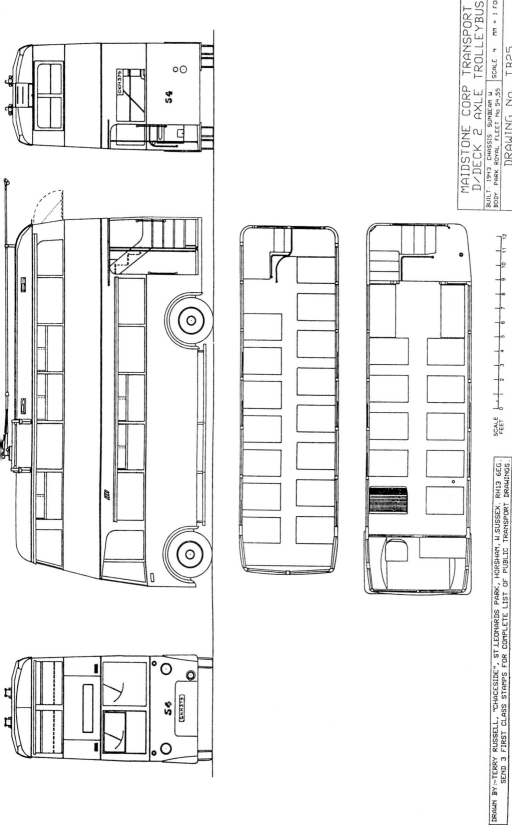

MAIDSTONE CORP TRANSPORT
D/DECK 2 AXLE TROLLEYBUS

BUILT: 1943 CHASSIS SUNBEAM W | SCALE 4 | MM = 1 FOOT
BODY PARK ROYAL FLEET No 54,55

DRAWING No TB25

SCALE
FEET
0 1 2 3 4 5 6 7 8 9 10 11 12

DRAWN BY:-TERRY RUSSELL, "CHACESIDE", ST LEONARDS PARK, HORSHAM, W.SUSSEX. RH13 6EG.
SEND 3 FIRST CLASS STAMPS FOR COMPLETE LIST OF PUBLIC TRANSPORT DRAWINGS.

54

GKN 579

102. Trolley 58 is seen again in September 1953 and it is wearing a predominantly brown livery. In this utility form each vehicle seated 30 on the top deck and 26 on the bottom. Trolleybuses 54 and 55 were delivered in 1943 and were registered GKN 379-380; 56 to 58 were registered GKP 511-513. (G.Druce)

103. In 1959/60 all the 54 to 58 series were rebodied by Charles H.Roe Ltd.; here on the left we see 54 in its final form. The rebodied vehicles seated 34 in the upper saloon and 28 in the lower. Trolleybus 56 was later preserved. (L.W.Rowe)

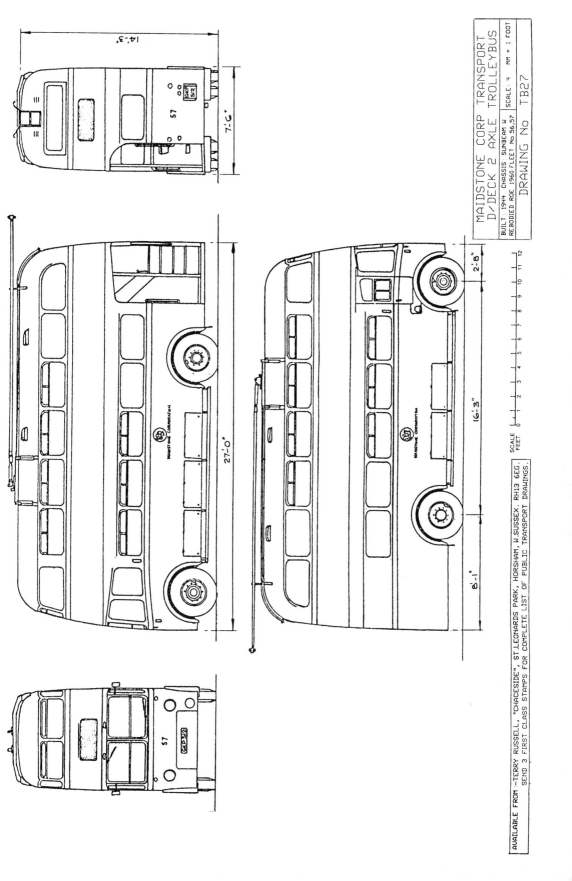

MAIDSTONE CORP TRANSPORT
D/DECK 2 AXLE TROLLEYBUS

BUILT 1944 CHASSIS SUNBEAM W
REBODIED ROE 1960 FLEET No 56.57

SCALE: 4   MM = : FOOT

DRAWING No TB27

14'-3"

7'-6"

27'-0"

16'-3"

2'-6"

8'-1"

SCALE
FEET   0 1 2 3 4 5 6 7 8 9 10 11 12

SKP 512

57

57

SKP 512

MAIDSTONE CORPORATION

MAIDSTONE CORPORATION

AVAILABLE FROM:- TERRY RUSSELL, "CHACESIDE", ST LEONARDS PARK, HORSHAM, W.SUSSEX. RH13 6EG.
SEND 3 FIRST CLASS STAMPS FOR COMPLETE LIST OF PUBLIC TRANSPORT DRAWINGS.

104. The Sunbeam Company also supplied the next batch of trolleybuses in 1946/7. They were numbered 62 to 73 and registered HKR 1-12. As can be seen here they were originally turned out in a mainly white livery, which certainly made an impact on the town. (W.J.Haynes)

105. In 1953 when this shot of 71 was taken, the livery had been toned down somewhat. Seating was for 30 on the top deck and 26 in the lower saloon. (G.Druce)

106. The final livery shows some of the changes introduced from 1954/5 onwards. The main brown colour has been altered to a golden ochre shade and cream has replaced white round the window frames. Trolleybus 72 was later preserved. (R.Cook Coll.)

107. Trolleybuses 83 and 84 were acquired secondhand from Llanelli; they were constructed in 1945 and seated 30 in the upper saloon and 26 in the lower. In 1955 these utility vehicles entered service in Maidstone. They were registered CBX 532-533 and were scrapped in 1961. (J.H.Meredith)

108. LCD 51-52 were former Brighton Corporation vehicles, manufactured by British United Traction and acquired by Maidstone in 1959. They seated 30 on the top deck and 26 on the bottom deck. Here we see 52 which retains its BUT makers plate above the fleet number. It has also yet to be fitted with its distinctive "goldfish" front grill. This vehicle was later preserved and can be seen at the East Anglian Transport Museum near Carlton Colville.   (L.W.Rowe)

109. The last trolleybuses bought by the
Corporation were the ex-Hastings vehicles
numbered 85 to 89 and registered BDY 807, 809,
810, 817 and 818. They were originally built by
Sunbeam in 1947/8. They had the usual 30 seats
on the top deck and 26 in the lower saloon. This
picture shows 88 in final condition; 86 was later
preserved.   (L.W.Rowe)

110. The date is 6th August 1956 and the overhead near the Wheatsheaf needs a little attention from a couple of linesmen standing on the tower wagon, a Tilling-Stevens which was later withdrawn in 1960. The overhead line crew originally consisted of three men, but from April 1958 more staff were required as the department took over responsibility for street lighting maintenance. (L.W.Rowe)

TOURS AND SPECIAL OCCASIONS

111. The flags are out along the High Street and one of the Ransomes vehicles supplies a grandstand view for several top deck passengers. This "top deck" view of the town was sorely missed, when in the 1970s the local authority went in for single deckers in a big way! (R.Cook Coll.)

112. Because of its compact size, attractive location and friendly management, the town attracted visits from several clubs and societies of transport enthusiasts. One of these visits was on 14th March 1948 when the Southern Counties Touring Society was hosted by the Corporation. Here some of the tour participants pose in front of one of the newly delivered trolleybuses of the 62 to 73 series. (J.Turley)

113. Another SCTS tour was on 4th March 1956 when we observe ex-Llanelli trolleybus 83 parked outside the Wheatsheaf. The gentleman on the right is Mr.Harrison, the Traffic Superintendent. Note the cramped conditions on the top deck! (J.H.Meredith)

114. As the 1950s drew to a close, abandonment of many of the country's trolleybus systems was already in process. Thus it was with particular satisfaction that a tour could be organised over a new extension, before it was officially opened to the public. Here at Park Wood on 12th April 1959, we see 51 disgorging its passengers on what seems to be a typically wild and windy spring day. (J.H.Meredith)

115. The Maidstone Corporation Transport Department celebrated its sixtieth anniversary in 1964. Trolleybus 66 was suitably decorated for the occasion and appeared on regular services. It is seen here in Mill Street as a Maidstone & District single decker, bound for Faversham, edges out of Palace Avenue. (L.W.Rowe)

116. We catch up with 66 again, this time on Loose Road. (T.Russell)

117. The motor bus side of the department gained in importance throughout the 1950s, and this view taken in March 1956 might be deemed an ominous sign for the trolleybuses. In St.Andrew's Road, Barming, WKP 71 poses in newly delivered state. In the background an M&D double decker passes one of the Tonbridge Road trolleybuses. (J.H.Meredith)

FAREWELL TO THE TROLLEYBUSES

118. A young Bob Cook pays a personal farewell to a much loved form of transport. Here at the Bull Inn, Barming, trolleybus 58 is restrained from running Bob over by a strategically placed chock wedged under the front wheel! (R.Cook)

119. Not many hours to go and an increase in carcinogenic diesel fumes is imminent. The trolleys had many supporters, but the council was seduced by the siren song of Leyland Motors, and HKR 11 was designated the last ceremonial vehicle. Here it is at Wren's Cross on the last day.   (J.E.Gready)

120. JOURNEYS END says the indicator blind as 72 enters the depot after a tour on 9th April 1967. Six days later it was all over, and work started on dismantling the overhead - never again would Maidstone folk "catch the trolley".   (J.H.Meredith)

Middleton Press

Easebourne Lane, Midhurst, West Sussex. GU29 9AZ Tel: 01730 813169 Fax: 01730 812601

...WRITE OR PHONE FOR OUR LATEST LIST...

BRANCH LINES
Branch Line to Allhallows
Branch Lines to Alton
Branch Lines around Ascot
Branch Line to Ashburton
Branch Lines around Bodmin
Branch Line to Bude
Branch Lines around Canterbury
Branch Line to Cheddar
Branch Lines to East Grinstead
Branch Lines to Effingham Junction
Branch Line to Fairford
Branch Line to Hawkhurst
Branch Line to Hayling
Branch Lines to Horsham
Branch Line to Ilfracombe
Branch Lines to Longmoor
Branch Line to Lyme Regis
Branch Line to Lynton
Branch Lines around Midhurst
Branch Line to Minehead
Branch Lines to Newport (IOW)
Branch Line to Padstow
Branch Lines around Plymouth
Branch Lines around Portmadoc 1923-46
Branch Lines around Porthmadog 1954-94
Branch Lines to Seaton & Sidmouth
Branch Line to Selsey
Branch Lines around Sheerness
Branch Line to Southwold
Branch Line to Swanage
Branch Line to Tenterden
Branch Lines to Torrington
Branch Line to Upwell
Branch Lines around Wimborne

SOUTH COAST RAILWAYS
Ashford to Dover
Brighton to Eastbourne
Chichester to Portsmouth
Dover to Ramsgate
Portsmouth to Southampton
Ryde to Ventnor
Worthing to Chichester

SOUTHERN MAIN LINES
Bromley South to Rochester
Charing Cross to Orpington
Crawley to Littlehampton
Dartford to Sittingbourne
East Croydon to Three Bridges
Epsom to Horsham
Exeter to Barnstaple
Exeter to Tavistock
Faversham to Dover
Haywards Heath to Seaford
London Bridge to East Croydon
Orpington to Tonbridge
Sittingbourne to Ramsgate
Swanley to Ashford
Tavistock to Plymouth
Victoria to Bromley South

Waterloo to Windsor
Woking to Portsmouth
Woking to Southampton
Yeovil to Exeter

COUNTRY RAILWAY ROUTES
Bath to Evercreech Junction
Bournemouth to Evercreech Jn.
Burnham to Evercreech Junction
Croydon to East Grinstead
East Kent Light Railway
Fareham to Salisbury
Frome to Bristol
Guildford to Redhill
Porthmadog to Blaenau
Reading to Basingstoke
Reading to Guildford
Redhill to Ashford
Salisbury to Westbury
Strood to Paddock Wood
Taunton to Barnstaple
Westbury to Bath
Woking to Alton

GREAT RAILWAY ERAS
Ashford from Steam to Eurostar
Festiniog in the Fifties
Festiniog in the Sixties

LONDON SUBURBAN RAILWAYS
Caterham and Tattenham Corner
Clapham Jn. to Beckenham Jn.
Crystal Palace and Catford Loop
East London Line
Holborn Viaduct to Lewisham
Lines around Wimbledon
London Bridge to Addiscombe
Mitcham Junction Lines
North London Line
South London Line
West Croydon to Epsom
West London Line
Willesden Junction to Richmond
Wimbledon to Epsom

STEAM PHOTOGRAPHERS
O.J.Morris's Southern Railways 1919-59

STEAMING THROUGH
Steaming through Cornwall
Steaming through East Sussex
Steaming through the Isle of Wight
Steaming through Kent
Steaming through West Hants
Steaming through West Sussex

TRAMWAY CLASSICS
Aldgate & Stepney Tramways
Barnet & Finchley Tramways
Bath Tramways
Bournemouth & Poole Tramways
Brighton's Tramways

Bristol's Tramways
Camberwell & W.Norwood Tramways
Croydon's Tramways
Clapham & Streatham Tramways
Dover's Tramways
East Ham & West Ham Tramways
Eltham & Woolwich Tramways
Embankment & Waterloo Tramways
Exeter & Taunton Tramways
Gosport & Horndean Tramways
Greenwich & Dartford Tramways
Hampstead & Highgate Tramways
Hastings Tramways
Holborn & Finsbury Tramways
Ilford & Barking Tramways
Kingston & Wimbledon Tramways
Lewisham & Catford Tramways
Maidstone & Chatham Tramways
North Kent Tramways
Portsmouth's Tramways
Reading Tramways
Seaton & Eastbourne Tramways
Southampton Tramways
Southend-on-sea Tramways
Southwark & Deptford Tramways
Stamford Hill Tramways
Thanet's Tramways
Victoria & Lambeth Tramways
Walthamstow & Leyton Tramways
Wandsworth & Battersea Tramways

TROLLEYBUS CLASSICS
Croydon's Trolleybuses
Hastings Trolleybuses
Maidstone Trolleybuses
Woolwich & Dartford Trolleybuses

WATERWAY ALBUMS
Hampshire Waterways
Kent and East Sussex Waterways
London's Lost Route to the Sea
London to Portsmouth Waterway
Surrey Waterways

MILITARY BOOKS
Battle over Portsmouth
Battle over Sussex 1940
Blitz over Sussex 1941-42
Bombers over Sussex 1943-45
Bognor at War
Military Defence of West Sussex
Secret Sussex Resistance

OTHER BOOKS
Brickmaking in Sussex
Garraway Father & Son
Index to all Stations
Industrial Railways of the South East
London Chatham & Dover Railway

SOUTHERN RAILWAY VIDEO
War on the Line